101374

D0431610

Bullying and Sexual Harassment

A practical handbook

TINA STEPHENS
AND
JANE HALLAS

Chandos Publishing
Oxford · England

Published in association with

Institute of Leadership
& Management

Chandos Publishing (Oxford) Limited
Chandos House
5 & 6 Steadys Lane
Stanton Harcourt
Oxford OX29 5RL
UK
Tel: +44 (0) 1865 884447 Fax: +44 (0) 1865 884448
Email: info@chandospublishing.com
www.chandospublishing.com

First published in Great Britain in 2006

ISBN:
1 84334 207 3 (paperback)
1 84334 208 1 (hardback)
978 1 84334 207 6 (paperback)
978 1 84334 208 3 (hardback)

© T. Stephens and J. Hallas, 2006

Typeset by Domex e-Data Pvt. Ltd.

Printed in the UK by 4edge Limited - www.4edge.co.uk

Contents

List of figures and tables

Figures

Tables

Table of cases

About the authors

Tina Stephens is a successful manager, tutor, writer, broadcaster and consultant. A mixture of roles as a personnel professional and a line manager has made her only too aware of the challenges that the day-to-day management of people presents. A partner and principal consultant with SandS Management Development Professionals, Tina delivers seminars and workshops on many aspects of managerial behaviour and is particularly keen to blend research and theory with a practical, down-to-earth approach to help those at the 'sharp end'. She is a Chartered Fellow of the CIPD.

The author may be contacted at:

E-mail: *tinastephens@btopenworld.com*
Tel: 01352 714005

Jane Hallas is a director of equalta based in North Wales and Buckinghamshire. She works with a range of organisations within both the public and private sectors, providing training and consultancy principally in employment law, diversity and equal opportunities. Jane also sits as an Employment Tribunal member and as an independent arbitrator for ACAS. She is a qualified mediator, specialising in improving poor working relationships through the mediation process. Jane also undertakes confidential bullying and harassment investigations for organisations. She is a member of the Industrial Law

Society and the Discrimination Law Association and an affiliate member of the Chartered Institute of Personnel and Development.

The author may be contacted at:

E-mail: *jane.hallas@equalta.co.uk*
Web: *www.equalta.co.uk*
Tel: 01978 356121

1

What is BASH?

Bullying and sexual harassment (BASH) are not easy to define in concise terms. Definitions and examples of what constitutes such behaviour are many and varied. The guiding principles though are that this behaviour is both unwelcome and persistent. The dictionary tells us that to harass is 'to annoy often' or 'to make sudden attacks on'. Tim Field offers two very comprehensive definitions:

> Persistent, unwelcome, intrusive behaviour of one or more individuals whose actions prevent others from fulfilling their duties. (Field, 1996)

> Repeatedly attacking someone verbally or physically with the intent of causing hurt, humiliation, belittlement, isolation and discrimination. (Field, n.d.)

Bullying and harassment may involve individuals or groups of individuals and, in terms of the traditional organisational hierarchy, it is no respecter of status. The manager (boss) may bully the subordinate, the subordinate may harass the boss and colleagues may bully or harass each other individually or in groups. Even when symptoms become obvious the difficulty lies in unearthing the causes and eradicating them.

The report from the Chartered Institute of Personnel Development (CIPD) on *Managing Conflict at Work* (2004) states:

> People can be subject to harassment for many reasons, including their:
> - race, ethnic origin, nationality or skin colour
> - gender or sexual orientation
> - age or youth
> - religious or political convictions
> - inability or unwillingness to assert themselves.
>
> (CIPD, 2004)

This book deals with the two forms of harassment that are most prevalent in all workplaces: bullying and sexual harassment. As acts of harassment, they have much in common: the victims are very vulnerable and often reluctant to complain, particularly as they may fear reprisals. Usually they just want the behaviour to stop.

Such harassment is not a new phenomenon but it is receiving much greater attention because of an increasingly diverse workforce and changing attitudes to equal opportunities and to what is acceptable behaviour at work.

The signs and symptoms of harassment are many and varied; illness, absenteeism, poor performance or resigning from the job are the most obvious. These signs and symptoms will have an effect on the lives of individuals at work and at home, as illustrated in Table 1.1. The table shows the major impact areas, though, of course, all problems at work are always likely to have some impact on home life eventually.

Harassment may be present in the form of:

- violence
- deliberately ignoring someone

Table 1.1   Impact of harassment

	Impact at work	Impact at home
Fear	✓	✓
Stress	✓	✓
Anxiety	✓	✓
Illness	✓	✓
Absenteeism	✓	
Apparent lack of commitment	✓	
Poor performance	✓	
Resigning from the job	✓	✓
Conflict	✓	✓
Poor morale	✓	✓
High labour turnover	✓	
Reduced productivity	✓	
Low efficiency	✓	
Accidents	✓	✓
Reduced quality	✓	
Divided teams	✓	

- jokes
- offensive language
- gossip
- slander
- sectarian songs or rhymes
- stalking
- unfounded criticism
- setting unattainable targets at work
- posters
- graffiti

- obscene gestures
- coercion for sexual favours
- pestering
- spying
- sarcasm.

Cases of bullying and harassment that reach the public eye through the media are usually those where a tribunal case or national survey has elicited the revelation of graphic, sometimes sensationalised, detail. These, however, are only a very small tip of a very large iceberg. Organisations that conduct their own workplace surveys are few and are usually shocked by what they discover.

Bullying is not always a sudden burst of temper resulting in a one-off instance of verbal or physical abuse. It is persistent and frequently includes the misuse of power gained from the bully's status in the organisation. It may be hidden from public view, though more often it would seem to involve acts of public humiliation.

Tim Field describes bullying as a form of violence: 'It's aggression expressed psychologically rather than physically – it's harmful. It can be more devastating than a physical injury and is compounded by denial and unenlightenedness' (Field, 1996).

A bully is someone who unfairly uses his or her size and strength to hurt or frighten weaker persons. That size and strength does not of course have to be physical. Status and power in the work environment can amount to the same thing. The focus for bullying is actually rarely based on gender, race or disability: it is more likely to feature the competence, or rather the alleged incompetence, of the victim. It can be typified in this comment received on the TUC 'Bad Bosses Hotline':

> My ex-boss used to manage his staff by humiliation. He would make people who did not reach the impossible targets he set stand in the corner wearing a dunce's hat ... Staff were terrified – some of them literally jumped every time he walked into the room.

Sexual harassment may take many forms: it can be verbal, non-verbal or physical. Examples include unsolicited sexual advances and propositions, lewd comments and innuendo, pornographic or sexually suggestive pictures or written materials, and physical contact with another employee.

It is well known that many people meet their future partner at work and indeed that intimate relationships, proper and improper, can flourish in the works canteen, at the drinks dispenser or in the store cupboard. It is only when such behaviour is unsolicited and unwelcome that it becomes sexual harassment. This in itself can cause a dilemma because victims often do not come forward, and even if they do, the harasser may declare lack of intention. 'Just being friendly', 'only a bit of a laugh' are common protestations and denials.

Though there have been cases where one incident has been sufficiently serious to warrant a justifiable complaint, sexual attention usually becomes classified as harassment if it persists and it has been made clear that it is regarded by the recipient as offensive and unwanted. As with bullying, the behaviour may be hidden and secretive, but it may instead be public, with the result that it embarrasses and humiliates the victim even more. Workplace harassment can be combated and resolved not only by developing and implementing preventive policies and procedures but also by ensuring an organisational culture and management style that fosters openness, trust and support.

Organisations conducting anonymous attitude surveys may be surprised to find significant allegations of bullying or sexual harassment and will need to be prepared to deal with them! Employers who receive few or no complaints about harassment should not be complacent. Remember, one crucial dilemma for the victim in these circumstances is whether or not to blow the whistle for fear of reprisal and further victimisation. The individual may be very reluctant to come forward, even to get the unwanted behaviour stopped. Even then, the spectre of involvement in subsequent investigations, disciplinary and even legal proceedings may be too daunting for many employees, who really just want to get on with their jobs and their lives.

So it's your problem now! You need to discover the size of that problem and begin to tackle it now!

As a personnel professional or a line manager you have several important responsibilities, including contributing to the success of your organisation in achieving its business objectives and maintaining the dignity and quality of working life for the people it employs. These responsibilities must be taken seriously. The short-term and long-term implications of missing or underperforming members of the workforce are crucial to the business.

It is your challenge to raise awareness and facilitate any changes that need to be made.

2

Why is this the manager's responsibility?

You could be breaking the law

There is now a range of legislation and quasi-legislation (e.g. Codes of Practice) which directly or indirectly relate to bullying and sexual harassment. As with much of our employment legislation, we find a mixture originating from both Brussels and Westminster, with case law 'fleshing out' statutes. It is worth remembering the old maxim: 'Ignorance of the law is no defence.' Therefore it is important for all employers, managers and supervisors to be aware of the law and the potential penalties for failing to protect employees from bullying or harassment.

The main sources of law relating to bullying and sexual harassment are:

- Sex Discrimination Act 1975, as amended;
- Protection from Harassment Act 1997;
- Employment Rights Act 1996, as amended;
- Public Interest Disclosure Act 1998;
- EC Council Directive 26/207 (Equal Treatment);
- EC Recommendation and Code of Practice on Protecting the Dignity of Women and Men at Work 1991;

- Equal Treatment Framework Directive 2000/78/EC;
- Equal Treatment Amendment Directive 2002/73/EC;
- Employment Act 2002.

Sometimes cases will involve other types of unlawful discrimination, including disability, race, sexual orientation or religion (and from 2006 age discrimination). Although beyond the scope of this book, the following statutes may also be relevant in harassment and bullying cases:

- Race Relations Act 1976, as amended;
- Disability Discrimination Act 1995, as amended;
- Employment Equality (Sexual Orientation) Regulations 2003;
- Employment Equality (Religion or Belief) Regulations 2003.

In addition to the above, it is possible to bring claims under the Criminal Justice and Public Order Act 1994 and common law claims for personal injury and breach of contract. A breach of contract claim could arise, for example, where a policy or procedure on bullying and harassment had contractual force and was found to be broken by the employer. Alternatively, if the employer denies the employee a prompt and reasonable opportunity for them to raise a grievance about bullying or harassment this could amount to a breach of the implied term of mutual trust and confidence. There may also be liability for negligence where the employee has developed serious mental ill health due to bullying at work.

There could be implications under the Health and Safety at Work Act 1974 regarding a failure to provide a safe working environment or safe system of working. Also worth noting are the new Health and Safety Executive Management Standards for Tackling Work Related Stress 2005. While these do not expressly refer to bullying, the standard on 'Working Relationships' refers to 'promoting positive working to avoid conflict and dealing with unacceptable behaviour'. The standards are not legally binding but following them will help organisations meet their legal duties.

The Protection from Harassment Act 1997 contains both civil and criminal sanctions, including making it a criminal offence to harass another or pursue a course of conduct which causes another to fear that violence will be used. These mostly apply to the more extreme cases of harassment, such as stalking.

It is far more likely that an employee will bring a claim under the Sex Discrimination Act for sexual harassment or the Employment Rights Act for bullying.

What is the legal definition of sexual harassment?

The EC Recommendation and Code of Practice on Protecting the Dignity of Women and Men at Work is not legally binding 'but should be taken into account by national courts'. Article 1 refers to conduct which is 'unwanted, unreasonable and offensive to the recipient' and which 'creates an intimidating, hostile or humiliating work environment for the recipient'. Article 2 requires member states to 'create a climate at work in which men and women respect one another's dignity'.

It is perhaps surprising that at the time of writing there is no UK statutory definition of sexual harassment. Instead claims need to be brought under the direct discrimination provisions of the Sex Discrimination Act in which direct discrimination is defined in s.1(1)(a) as where 'a person discriminates against a woman if on the ground of her sex he treats her less favourably than he treats or would treat a man.'

One of the earliest cases, *Strathclyde Regional Council v. Porcelli* (1986) determined that a woman who had been subjected to a series of inappropriate acts and comments by two male colleagues with the aim of making her leave could claim successfully under the Act. The Court of Session recognised that their behaviour was directed at her *as a woman* and they would not have treated a man in the same way.

Under the legislation it is the *treatment* of the claimant that needs to be proved, not the intention or motive of the defendant to discriminate. Once a complainant has established prima facie facts from which an Employment Tribunal believes discrimination can be inferred, the burden of proof shifts to the employer to prove that, on a balance of probabilities, they did *not* commit the alleged harassment. Of course, a man can also bring a claim under the Act as any references to 'woman' in the Act can be replaced by 'man' and vice versa.

Sexual harassment as a detriment

Under the Act it is unlawful for a person, in the case of a woman employed by him at an establishment in Great Britain, to discriminate against her by dismissing her or subjecting her to any other *detriment*. Case law has established sexual harassment is capable of amounting to a detriment. However, according to *Bahl v. Law Society* (2004) (a case about direct sex discrimination, not harassment) bad treatment alone is insufficient to succeed in a claim for direct sex discrimination; there has to be *worse* treatment when viewed on a comparative basis.

In *BT plc v. Williams* (1997) the Employment Appeal Tribunal (EAT) defined sexual harassment as 'unwanted conduct of a personal nature or other conduct based on sex affecting the dignity of women and men at work.' The case also recognised that sexual harassment is gender-specific, so that the claimant need not show that she has been treated less favourably than a man.

However, the House of Lords in the leading (joined) case of *MacDonald* v. *Advocate General for Scotland; Pearce* v. *Governing Body of Mayfield Secondary School* (2003) took the opportunity to take a considered look at sexual harassment and essentially reverted to the basic language under the Act. Having considered the previous case law, they decided that there had to be a comparator, whether real or actual. This suggests that if the employer can show that they would have treated a man equally badly, there is no sex discrimination. They also confirmed that sexual harassment within the meaning of the Sex Discrimination Act applies if the reason behind the misbehaviour is connected with the *victim's sex*.

Therefore harassment is likely to impose a detriment if, for example, uncouth or crude and smutty language of a sexual nature is used – more so if this situation is compounded by inappropriate bodily contact. However, it is insufficient to be subjected to insulting behaviour per se; it needs to be related to the person's gender.

It is important to note that a remark can amount to a detriment even if not made to the woman herself but to others. In *Hereford and Worcester County Council* v. *Clayton* (1996) a fire brigade divisional officer said to his watch: 'The good news is that you are getting someone else for the watch, but the bad news is that it is a woman.'

While the *MacDonald* decision has perhaps narrowed the scope for bringing a claim of sexual harassment, it must be noted that from October 2005 there will be specific statutory definitions of harassment and sexual harassment similar to the ones currently applicable for other types of discriminatory harassment which will hopefully take away the legal hoops through which the claimant currently has to jump.

Is the test subjective or objective?

According to the EAT in *Whitley* v. *Thompson* (1997) essentially it is for the woman to set the boundaries beyond which she finds certain behaviour unobjectionable and to make those boundaries clear. So if the objection to, or rejection of, the behaviour would be clear to a reasonable person, to continue with the behaviour would normally amount to harassment. In *Reed & Anor* v. *Stedman* (1999) it was stated that it is for the complainant to determine whether the behaviour is unacceptable and offensive to her.

It is perhaps understandable that many workplace policies have defined harassment purely in subjective terms, stating it is for the recipient to determine whether they think they have been harassed. However, this can cause problems where the claimant is particularly sensitive. In *Driskel* v. *Peninsula Business Services Ltd* (2000) the court took into account the alleged harasser's *reasonable* perception of their conduct and its impact on the recipient. There is thus both a subjective and objective element to sexual harassment; would a reasonable person find the behaviour unacceptable by normal standards of behaviour and did that complainant find it caused them upset?

How frequent do the incidents of sexual harassment have to be?

For cases of sexual harassment there does not necessarily have to be a series of acts to succeed in a claim of sexual harassment. A serious one-off act can be sufficient to constitute a detriment, according to the EAT in *Bracebridge Engineering Ltd* v. *Darby* (1990).

Does the complainant have to object to the harassment?

Case law suggests that tribunals are willing to recognise that it can be very difficult for a woman to object to sexual harassment when the harasser is in a senior position. The courts have recognised that certain types of behaviour can properly be regarded as being unacceptable without the woman having to make this explicit, for example touching a woman in a sexual way, unless, of course, the woman had expressly welcomed or initiated it.

There are, however, different degrees of behaviour where it is less obvious that they are unacceptable, for example suggestive e-mails, office banter and various forms of innuendo. In these situations it is advisable for the woman to make it clear she does not find them acceptable rather than to go along with them or remain silent.

What are the employer's/manager's responsibilities?

Responsibility under s.41, Sex Discrimination Act 1975, is described thus:

> Anything done by a person in the course of his employment shall be treated as done by his employer as well as by him, whether or not it was done with the employer's knowledge or approval.

In *Jones* v. *Tower Boot Co. Ltd* (1997) the employer was said to be responsible for acts of employees within the

13

workplace, unless the actions clearly go beyond the employer's control.

The House of Lords in *Waters* v. *Metropolitan Police Commissioner* (2000) stated '... the employer will not be liable unless he knows or ought to know that the harassment is taking place and fails to take reasonable steps to prevent it.'

The (in)famous case of *Burton and Rhule* v. *De Vere Hotels* (1996) (the Bernard Manning case) established liability emanating from third parties where the employer fails to take adequate steps to protect his employees from harassment. This case has now been overruled by *Pearce* (above). The Law Lords said that *Burton* had gone too far; the failure to take reasonable steps to prevent an employee from suffering harassment was discrimination only where the *reason* for that failure to act amounted to sex or race discrimination.

Is there a defence to a claim of sexual harassment?

The defence under s.41(3), Sex Discrimination Act 1975, to a claim of sexual harassment is that the employer 'took such steps as were reasonably practicable to prevent the employee from doing that act or from doing in the course of his employment acts of that description.'

Reasonably practicable steps are set out in the EC Recommendation and Code of Practice and include:

- having a written statement or policy on sexual harassment;
- ensuring that the statement or policy is communicated to all employees;
- taking responsibility for creating a workplace environment which protects employees' dignity;

- enabling employees to bring a complaint of harassment by providing advice and assistance;
- encouraging problems to be dealt with informally initially;
- investigating properly any complaints of harassment;
- taking appropriate disciplinary action for breaching anti-harassment policies;
- training all managers on how to deal with sexual harassment.

Forthcoming changes to the definition of sexual harassment

As explained above, it is important to note that the definition of sexual harassment will change in October 2005 when the amended version of the Equal Treatment Directive is implemented in the UK. For the first time, there will be a specific, free-standing right not to be sexually harassed.

The amended wording of the Equal Treatment Directive 2002/73/EC defines *harassment* as:

> Where an unwanted conduct related to the sex of a person occurs with the purpose or effect of violating the dignity of a person, and of creating an intimidating, hostile, degrading, humiliating or offensive environment.

This wording reflects the definition used for other forms of harassment, that is race, disability, sexual orientation, religion and belief and age discrimination.

There is also a separate definition of *sexual harassment*:

> Where any form of unwanted verbal, non-verbal or physical conduct of a sexual nature occurs, with the

purpose or effect of violating the dignity of a person, in particular when creating an intimidating, hostile, degrading, humiliating or offensive environment.

Harassment and sexual harassment within the meaning of this Directive shall be deemed to be discrimination on the grounds of sex and therefore prohibited. A person's rejection of, or submission to, such conduct may not be used as a basis for a decision affecting that person.

The two definitions recognise that some men may harass women simply because they are women, but it is not sexually based. This could include, for example, derogatory remarks about them as women but containing no sexual connotations. Others forms of harassment may have sexual under (and over-) tones; this would include lewd comments (verbal), displaying pornographic images or sending sexually explicit text messages (non-verbal) or brushing up against a woman or touching her in an inappropriate manner (physical).

There are likely to be a number of benefits for claimants from this new definition. One is that they will no longer have to show a comparison with how a man would be treated. A second is that the complainant will not have to establish that they suffered a detriment.

What about bullying?

There is no law which specifically prohibits bullying of employees. Instead successful claims have been brought by employees claiming that they have been constructively dismissed. Constructive dismissal means the employer has behaved in such a way as to fundamentally breach the employee's contract of employment so that the employee has no option but to resign. The most common claim is that the employer has breached the implied term of mutual trust and confidence. This could include bullying by a manager or failure to protect an employee from being bullied by others at work. This is clearly far from ideal as it means that things have to get so bad that the employee is forced into resigning.

The employee will normally have to show a series of acts which culminated in his or her resignation. A series of trivial acts can add up to a fundamental breach of contract, for example persistent criticism or humiliation in front of others designed to undermine the employee over time. Nor does the last act complained of have to be fundamental, provided it is the 'straw which breaks the camel's back'.

Employers also have an implied contractual duty to provide employees with reasonable support against bullying by colleagues, customers and members of the public.

In bringing a constructive dismissal claim the employee will be taking action for unfair constructive dismissal under the Employment Rights Act. This means there will be a cap on the maximum compensation they can claim. For 2005 this is £56,800. This should be contrasted with the unlimited compensation potentially available in sex discrimination claims.

Blowing the whistle

Compensation under the Public Interest Disclosure Act 1998 is now available for dismissal and victimisation for any employee who speaks out ('blows the whistle') against wrongdoing in the workplace, provided that certain conditions are met. While most of the instances involve the disclosure of confidential information, bullying and harassment practices which may have become institutionalised through the culture could still be included.

For protection, the disclosure must consist of information which tends to show one or more of the following:

- a criminal offence;
- failure to comply with a legal obligation;
- a miscarriage of justice;
- danger to the health and safety of an individual;
- damage to the environment;
- the deliberate concealment of information relating to the above.

The employee is protected if a qualifying disclosure is made in good faith to his/her employer or to another person when the employee reasonably believes the failure relates solely or mainly to the conduct of that person or to a matter for which that person has legal responsibility.

The Act also suggests that the employee can go to 'prescribed persons' such as health and safety representatives or the Health and Safety Executive. Additional requirements, such as not making the disclosure for payment and reasonably believing the disclosed information is substantially true, need to be met if the employee 'blows the whistle' in other circumstances (that is to other people apart from the employer or prescribed persons). The Act therefore affords some protection against dismissal or detriment provided the employee has made a protected disclosure.

So what must I do as a manager?

An employer *must* investigate complaints. Failure to deal with a complaint may amount to a breach of trust and confidence, and therefore neglect of the employer's duty of care, as the following case illustrates (*Hatrick* v. *City Fax*, OIT 3041/138):

Case Study

An employee [Ms Hatrick] had her hair forcibly cut by a colleague. She was distressed and reported the incident to the personnel manager. Management decided to take no action over what they considered to be a minor act of stupidity because it might escalate the situation. The tribunal thought that employees were entitled to expect protection from this sort of behaviour.

Any reasonable employee would have had her confidence shaken if her employer had decided to take no action when faced with 'a blatant case of horseplay or bullying', and a reasonable employer would have responded immediately to the complaint.

The employer's failure to act was a fundamental breach of contract entitling Ms Hatrick to resign and claim constructive dismissal.

It is also important that if a complaint is investigated and upheld, any subsequent disciplinary action complies, as a minimum, with the new statutory disciplinary and dismissal procedure implemented in October 2004. Failure to do so could lead to a finding of automatically unfair dismissal.

What will bullying and sexual harassment cost the organisation?

Potential direct costs

According to the CIPD:

Conflict at work costs employers nearly 450 days of management time each year – equivalent to the time of two managers full time – and almost 4% of grievance and disciplinary cases are related to bullying or harassment incidents.

The CIPD's report *Managing Conflict at Work* (2004) states that on average *12.8 days* per year are spent preparing for employment tribunals, including management, HR staff and lawyers' time.

The same report looks at the average costs associated with employment tribunals (see Table 2.1).

| Table 2.1 | Average costs associated with employment tribunals |

Costs	UK average £
Settling tribunals out of court	2,063
Paying compensation awarded by tribunals	650
Legal advice	3,021
Recruiting replacements for staff who left due to a dispute	1,750

Source: CIPD (2004).

In addition to the employer being sued in a discrimination claim, it is possible that the perpetrator can be personally named as a respondent in the case, which could result in an award being made against them personally so they have to pay compensation to the victim.

However, the total costs are likely to be hidden in the potential indirect costs associated with bullying and harassment. This is even more so where a whole organisational culture is based on bullying.

Potential indirect costs

For the organisation, bullying and sexual harassment may lead to:

- poor performance management;
- increased absenteeism;
- high labour turnover;
- increased overtime;
- reduction in quality standards;
- missed deadlines;
- poor customer service;
- reduced employee morale;
- increased labour turnover;
- reduced customer satisfaction;
- increasing number of accidents;
- increased need for closer supervision;
- poor decision-making or a lengthening of the process;
- damaged reputation.

For the individual, suffering bullying and sexual harassment directly may lead to:

- poor performance leading to critical appraisals;
- action under disciplinary or capability procedures;
- loss of confidence;
- loss of livelihood;
- loss of income;
- damaged or destroyed career;
- separation and divorce;
- ill-health, including depression and even suicide.

For the individual who is not suffering directly from bullying and sexual harassment there is still a cost:

- extra work to cover for absent or underperforming colleagues;

- inability to carry out his or her own job because of underperformance or mistakes by others;

- accidents caused by others;

- poor working environment;

- loss of bonus.

These could eventually lead to colleagues suffering stress. The effect can be like falling dominoes.

Invest in anti-bullying and harassment training and the development of clear competency standards for managers. Just avoiding one serious case makes this a cost-effective arrangement.

3

What can I do about it?

Establishing a policy

One policy or several?

Any instance of sexual harassment or bullying will be easier to resolve if the organisation has an established policy and procedures for dealing with it.

Many organisations already have such mechanisms in place for issues of sexual harassment and use these to deal with bullying. In other instances equal opportunities or even grievance policy and procedures are used.

Policies used to deal with bullying

The CIPD report that 83 per cent of employers who responded to their 2004 *Managing Conflict at Work* survey claim to have an anti-bullying policy in place. This might be a separate policy or an all-inclusive harassment and bullying policy. Some organisations suggest that these issues are included in their equal opportunities policy.

Is our existing equal opportunities policy enough?

Where a policy for sexual harassment or equal opportunities is 'broadened' to include bullying, the name is often changed.

For example, it becomes a policy for 'maintaining dignity at work'. Just changing the title may not be enough, and if every new area of victimisation or other wrong treatment at work is going to be another paragraph in an existing policy, it is unlikely that the effect will be positive. This 'tagging on' process is better achieved by a review of the existing policy and procedures. The new areas of behaviour need to be fully integrated. It is even suggested that separate policy and procedures need to be established to deal with bullying.

In order of preference, you should have:

- separate policies for sexual harassment and bullying;
- bullying policy incorporated into sexual harassment policy;
- bullying and sexual harassment policies incorporated into equal opportunities policy;
- bullying and sexual harassment issues dealt with through grievance and disciplinary procedures.

No policy is perfect, but it will show everyone in the organisation that you are serious about the issues and that you will endeavour to:

- treat all cases fairly and quickly;
- do everything possible to eradicate such types of behaviour.

What is policy?

Organisations will have policies regarding most facets of their business. They provide:

- an expression of broad intentions;
- an expression of what to do in a given situation;
- an expression of organisational culture.

They also serve to:

- guide attitude;
- guide decisions;
- guide actions.

What's the best approach to policy for my organisation?

Depending on the size and nature of the organisation, the policy will fall somewhere along the following spectrum:

No policy – Assumed policy – Informal policy – Full, formal, explicit policy

The extent to which that policy is communicated will range from:

Covert ← → *Overt*

known by only a few and   published and
not committed to paper   available to all staff

The decision about where to put your organisation on this spectrum is not all that straightforward. Too full, explicit and overt might mean less flexibility and it is unlikely that any two cases of bullying and sexual harassment will be the same. Too covert, and there is likely to be inconsistency and indecision.

However, because this issue is such a sensitive one, and in order at best to discourage such behaviour and at least to encourage victims to come forward, then a more explicit approach is recommended.

Why does policy about bullying and sexual harassment need to be explicit?

An explicit policy will:

- provide all employees with indications of probable decisions that will be made in particular circumstances;

- express uniformity of intentions regarding employee demands for fairness and equity;

- provide predictability for repetitive situations;

- show that the management of the organisation has thought in advance how possible contingencies will be dealt with;

- enable top management to influence decisions at all levels;

- provide a framework within which it is easier to assess the effect of policy and, where necessary, to achieve change;

- give those formulating the policy experience of problem-solving;

- establish the limits on decisions to be taken by individual managers;

- ensure greater consistency.

How is policy made effective?

If the proper amount of time and energy is expended on putting the policy and procedures in place, then that in itself may dramatically reduce bullying and sexual harassment-related behaviour. To be effective the policy should be:

- stated in positive terms;

- in writing;

- widely distributed and publicised;

- applied fairly and uniformly;
- related to the ongoing business context;
- constantly updated.

Designing and drafting your bullying and sexual harassment policy

Have you:

- consulted widely inside and outside the organisation?

- got a clear statement from top management on how bullying and sexual harassment is viewed by the organisation?

- established a variety of means for publicity and awareness-raising?

- ensured that the procedure for dealing with complaints is confidential?

- ensured that the treatment of those accused is professional and sensitive?

- ensured that the procedure for dealing with complaints is quick but thorough, with a timescale for responses?

- trained staff to identify actual or potential problem situations?

- trained staff to counsel those involved?

- considered how to deal with the aftermath for both the victim and perpetrator?

- made it proactive?

- ensured that written records will be kept?

- made both individuals and managers responsible for their actions?

- provided examples of unacceptable behaviour?
- provided examples of good practice?

Who can help to put the right policy in place?

Externally:

- other employers locally or in your particular sector;
- professional bodies;
- trade unions;
- employer organisations;
- advisory services;
- publications.

Internally:

- using consultative committees or perhaps establishing these for the first time to deal with this issue;
- analysing the culture, structure and management style of the organisation to establish 'best fit';
- surveys.

When should I start?

Some organisations introduce their policy following cases in the workplace which may or may not have led to disciplinary action or legal proceedings. Some organisations are more proactive, following recommended best practice and learning from the painful and expensive experiences of others. *Being proactive is best.*

Examining organisational culture, structure and management style

The size, structure and culture of your organisation is worth examining to highlight potential causes of harassment or failure to deal with it. Organisations exist to pursue varied objectives and may operate in different ways, but none can justify the abuse of employees through harassment in the achievement of those objectives.

Culture

This has been best defined by Charles Handy in *Understanding Organisations* (1985) as 'the way we do things around here'.

Culture must be seen as a two-way process: it shapes the behaviour of all employees and they in turn shape the way the organisation performs. Different departments or sites in the same organisation may show cultural differences, and a healthy organisation will tolerate and absorb this. Culture includes deep-set beliefs about work organisation, authority, reward and control, and an understanding of culture is essential if any change process or procedure is envisaged.

This means that what might be 'acceptable' behaviour in one department or organisation would not be tolerated in another – offensive language, for example, or the frequent playing of practical jokes. It could be said that if all employees accept the culture, then even if it is inappropriate from a 'good practice' point of view it should be allowed to continue, but evidence has shown that although people do 'accept' the culture this may be because they need the job and are too scared to speak out. Ask yourself: 'Should the culture as it is, even if it is inappropriate from a good practice point of view, be allowed to continue if it breaks the law and treats individuals or groups without respect and dignity, or worse still, with degradation and humiliation?' In understanding the culture of your organisation some external 'good practice' benchmarking might be the way to determine the potential or actual existence of harassment and the choice of the best way to deal with it.

Structure

The structure of the organisation will dictate in particular where the power lies, and it is the abuse of power that so often leads to harassment. Autocracy will place the decision-making focus in the hands of the few. In a small organisation this may well be the owner only, and the treatment of people may be at a whim and without a two-way dialogue. If the owner/manager values employees, then harassment is unlikely. If he or she does not, then there may be little that can be done. Stemming from autocracy, in the bigger organisation bureaucracy will emerge. Power will continue to be held or focused centrally and the structure will spawn its own procedures and red tape to ensure strict control of behaviour. Both of these structures emphasise the elevation of the few above the many, and restrict any communication other than top-down.

Finally, a matrix may be the focus for the organisation, with power and authority constantly shifting as projects are completed and objectives met. Here leaders or 'bosses' are in their positions based on their given skills for a fixed period of time. A manager who is soon going to be a colleague again may have a different approach to the treatment of others!

Recently the delayering of many organisations has brought more decision-making power to different levels, and many managers act as mentors or coaches rather than as admirals or emperors. This in itself requires collaboration rather than confrontation and so should induce more harmonious working relationships.

Modern organisation structures are, in the main, flatter and leaner to make them more efficient. The decision-making is nearer the coal face and nearer the customer. Individuals at work are encouraged to monitor their own work and to make their own decisions. Project teams, drawn together from across the spectrum of the organisation, plan and organise. E-mails and intranets make communications direct and immediate. Though positive changes in many ways, these new ways of working may lead to uncertainty and conflict for managers and their staff. Managers in particular can become anxious and lose confidence as they move from telling and directing to asking and facilitating.

Management style

Management style will emerge from the structure and culture, and to be effective the three should show complementarity. With decision-making power in the hands of the few, an autocratic controlling management style will evolve, nothing being done if it doesn't please 'the boss'. No checks and balances, and top managers who are all of the same mind, will lead inevitably to the abuse of power and is a hotbed for breeding harassment.

Bureaucracy, too, could be dangerous, but this depends on what type of procedural red tape is present. It is fine if it has sound bullying and sexual harassment procedures, but not so if it really is 'bound', because all actions will be governed or even hidden by bureaucratic red tape.

A more democratic, involved, empowering style of management will make the manager (boss) much more accountable to his or her staff and much more transparent in his or her actions.

Managers may well be confused about their role and their legitimate use of 'power'. Have you reviewed their job descriptions? Have you trained them in 'new' management techniques? Incidences of 'pressure bullying' are on the increase caused by the work overload experienced by managers.

Managerial behaviour is influenced by five major sources:

- senior management;
- peers;
- themselves and their preferred approach;
- subordinates;
- customers.

The design of the manager's job needs to be reviewed to reveal any conflict or confusion. Once the role is better defined with parameters for acceptable and legitimate behaviour revealed to all staff, everyone can see where a manager is overstepping the line.

What can help to accommodate culture, structure and managerial style?

- Has your organisation become leaner and flatter?
- Have your managers had recent management training?
- Do senior managers understand the legal and financial implications of bullying and sexual harassment?
- Do your managers all 'sing to the same hymn sheet' when dealing with staff in what could be seen as a fair and respectful way?
- Do your employees understand the legitimate power and authority of the boss and the wider organisation in terms of what they can rightly expect to have said and done to them at work?

Power and authority

Inevitably linked with culture and management style is the use of power and authority in the organisation. Power is often abused in bullying and sexual harassment cases. It's important that you understand what it is and how it works.

Power may come through position, expertise or control over information or over other resources. It may also embrace or control other rewards and punishments. The chief executive is powerful, and so is the chief executive's secretary!

> Power lies in the acceptance of your authority by others, their knowledge that if they try to resist you they will fail and you will succeed. Real power does not lie in documents, it lies in what you can achieve. (Jay, 1967)

It is the use of power that can determine whether the manager is simply macho or oversteps the line and becomes a bully.

> Managers must possess a high need for power, that is, a concern for influencing people. However, this need must be disciplined and controlled so that it is directed towards the benefit of the institution as a whole and not towards the manager's personal aggrandisement. (McClelland and Burnham, 1976)

So the successful exercise of power requires:

- using power openly and legitimately;
- being sensitive to what types of power are most effective with different people;
- developing all sources of power and not relying on just one technique;

- seeking jobs and tasks which will give opportunity for the use of power;

- using power in a mature and self-controlled way, deriving satisfaction from influencing others.

Communicating the policy

At the design stage

First, awareness of the organisation's policy may be raised at the time of its design (or redesign). Using an existing group, e.g. a consultative committee or equal opportunities group, gives an excellent opportunity to discover what employees are looking for from the policy. Either of these groups is likely to be representative of the organisational cross-section.

Use their suggestions, add your external knowledge, and return to them and senior management during the development stage. A policy that has been jointly drawn up and designed is more likely to be accepted and adhered to. By the time the policy is written and accepted its existence and content should have become well known.

Once the policy and attendant procedures have been accepted there is a danger that the papers will pass to the desk drawer of the personnel manager, into the staff handbook and into the minutes of the working party by whom it was devised. Isn't that a good thing? Doesn't it mean that no harassment is taking place? Probably not – it just means it isn't being dealt with! The exercise has therefore been a complete waste of time.

Something as important as this needs to be flagged up as often as possible – it is surprising how such issues pass people by!

A huge flurry of excitement at its instigation is all well and good, but what about 12 months down the line? Any potential victim needs to know his or her rights but the bully or harasser may choose not to be familiar with the policy, thus claiming ignorance when involved in any investigation.

Who needs to know?

- New staff:
  - in letters of appointment;
  - in contracts of employment;
  - in the induction pack and programme.

- Existing staff:
  - on notice boards;
  - in newsletters;
  - in cloakrooms and changing rooms;
  - in the canteen and rest rooms;
  - in the staff handbook.

- Managers (as well as the general information that is available to all staff):
  - regular debriefing where bullying and harassment has occurred in any department;
  - regular reminders of the procedures and penalties.

- Contractors/suppliers:
  - make it part of the terms of the contract that the policy should be honoured;
  - encourage them to adopt similar policies.

What information do people need?

- The procedure
- The penalties
- The confidentiality and counselling available
- Names and locations and phone numbers of people to go to.

Consult, construct and agree a policy statement

This must show how the policy will:

- treat all cases fairly;
- maintain confidentiality;
- listen to all sides without jumping to conclusions;
- keep those involved aware of what progress is being made;
- get rid of the behaviour;
- be positive and proactive not reactive;
- emphasise that all cases will be thoroughly investigated;
- outline procedure and corrective action;
- set goals and improvement targets for dealing with the problem.

Use the policy!

Remember, this will include not only monitoring incidents but looking at the culture, structure and management style of the organisation. Are the norms acceptable? Can we use the excuse that 'this is the way we do things around here' if we are contravening legislation and damaging the dignity of people at work?

4

What procedures should we adopt and develop?

Complaints procedure

Be imaginative!

It is essential that a procedure is put into place to allow for any claims of bullying and harassment to be dealt with quickly, fairly, confidentially and objectively. All employees need ready access to that procedure without having to ask for a copy. Policies and procedures should be:

- visible;
- accessible.

It's a good idea to post copies, or at least the main points, in cloakrooms, canteens, rest rooms or other public places. They can also be made available on an intranet system if there is one. For larger organisations a poster campaign or other publicity initiatives can also be an effective way of getting the anti-bullying message across. Imaginative initiatives could include 'road shows' where the HR team go out and about their organisation, handing out leaflets, offering advice and guidance and generally raising the profile of the policy. Employees can also receive personal letters addressed to them at home explaining the anti-bullying stance and procedure. Ideally these should be signed by the most senior person within the organisation. Don't forget to provide alternative formats to meet the needs of disabled employees, for example making the procedure available in large type or on audio cassette.

Encouragement

In addition to this, employees must be encouraged to use the procedure, and it needs to be monitored and reviewed to ensure that it is working. It must allow employees to bypass line managers or supervisors who may be the cause for complaint. Standard grievance procedures are not considered to be a suitable means of dealing with bullying and sexual harassment because of the very personal and sometimes intimate and embarrassing nature of the offence.

This is particularly the case with sexual harassment, where normally grievances would first be raised with the line manager. Very often the line manager for a woman is a man (and of course there are a growing number of instances where the boss is female and the harassment is being suffered by a male subordinate). Some women may fear they will not be taken seriously and this may dissuade them from pursuing a complaint. Men may feel that they are demonstrating a weakness if they have to discuss the issue with their boss.

A two-stage procedure is recommended allowing for an initial informal resolution. Should that not resolve the issue then a formal procedure may be instigated.

Procedures and investigations

It is essential that any complaints procedure complies, as a minimum, with the statutory grievance procedure introduced by the Employment Act 2002. Appendix 1 contains guidance as to what is included in the standard three-step statutory procedure. It also provides checklists for the informal and formal stages and the investigation process.

Informal stage

Most victims of harassment simply want it to stop. It is therefore recommended that incidents are initially dealt with informally. The ACAS Code of Practice on disciplinary and grievance procedures advises employers to allow employees to resolve grievances of any type informally in the first instance. Ensuring that your procedure has an informal option allows people to try and resolve the problem before it escalates. Here the individual should be given the opportunity to discuss the complaint with a trained volunteer from the workforce or an outside agency commissioned by the employer to provide a support and guidance service. Their role is to listen and help the employee decide what to do. They must explore all possible courses of action the complainant may have, and give him or her the courage to raise the issue with the perpetrator, directly or through a third party, which may in itself settle the matter. The provision of a mobile phone for the trained volunteer helps to maintain confidentiality and gives employees more confidence.

In the words of the European Commission Code of Practice for the Protection of the Dignity of Women and Men at Work, employers are advised to 'designate someone to provide advice and assistance to employees subjected to sexual harassment where possible with responsibilities to assist in the resolution of any problems'. The formality of this role will vary between organisations, as demonstrated in Table 4.1. In some organisations all the roles in Table 4.1 will be enacted at varying stages in the procedure.

Table 4.1   Support role: degrees of formality

Volunteer	Adviser	Harassment officer	Professional counsellor (EAP)
Informal	Informal	Formal	Formal
Untrained	Part-trained/trained	Trained	Trained
Amateur	Volunteer		

The informal volunteer, or 'buddy', untrained in any 'professional' sense, will be a colleague possibly, or at least a peer. Organisations are fortunate if there are employees who are willing to help in this way but it is advisable that they are given some training to undertake the role.

The adviser will have more experience and training, while the harassment or equal opportunities officer may be in a formal post which includes not only helping victims, respondents and witnesses but also monitoring, evaluation, training and awareness-raising. The harassment or equal opportunities officer may be a full-time post in larger organisations, or form only part of someone's duties if the organisation is small.

The professional counsellor may be internal to the organisation or, commonly these days, part of an (external) employee assistance programme (EAP).

However informal and voluntary the level of support, it is essential that an individual in this role:

- understands bullying and harassment;
- is familiar with the organisation's procedure;
- is aware of legislation;
- is able to give information;
- is able to explain options;

- is able to help victims to understand that they can do something if they want to but are not under any pressure to do so;
- is able to talk with respondents and witnesses;
- is a good listener.

Formal stage

Making the complaint

The complainant makes a formal, written complaint identifying the bully or harasser. There is a time limit for settlement of complaints. If the complaint is not dealt with swiftly and decisively, the bullying or harassment will probably continue.

The complaint should be acknowledged in writing as soon as possible and the alleged bully/harasser given written notification of it at the same time, with full details of the allegations. Those involved in the complaint should not talk openly about it. In fact, some organisations suspend the accused on full pay for the period of the investigation. If an employee is suspended, it is important that this does not imply that the complaint is upheld, only that it is a precautionary measure while the investigation is conducted. Do remember though that this may cause the 'accused' individual great stress.

If a standard grievance procedure is used (although this is not recommended it may be the only practical method in a small business), it is important that there is a means of lodging a complaint with someone other than the supervisor or line manager. If the business is very small, the procedure could provide for an external person to come in and investigate such complaints. ACAS can provide lists of suitably qualified people or the various business and telephone directories available will usually contain listings of people who undertake such work.

For example, the bullying and harassment procedure for Delmar Worldchoice, a small independent travel agency, provides for the following:

> You should raise the matter with one of the Partners by putting your complaint in writing, setting out the details of your complaint and including dates, times and names of any witnesses. You can raise your grievance with **any** of the Partners in the business. Alternatively, if the complaint relates to a very sensitive issue, for example a complaint against one of the Partners, external investigators may be appointed to ensure an independent and unbiased investigation takes place.

Investigating the complaint

The complaint must be investigated promptly, preferably by someone outside the department where the parties involved work. For particularly sensitive or complex cases, including allegations against senior managers, it is advisable to consider appointing an external investigator. The investigator should be fully trained in handling these complaints.

- The complainant should be interviewed first.
- Evidence to corroborate the allegation should be identified, including dates and times of alleged incidents and names of potential witnesses.
- The alleged bully/harasser should be interviewed.
- All witnesses for both parties should be interviewed.
- Both parties should be represented if they wish, e.g. by a colleague or trade union representative.

If the complaint of bullying or harassment is raised at a time when disciplinary procedures are in force for some other reason, then the bullying/harassment complaint should take precedence and the disciplinary action be suspended temporarily.

How do we conduct the interview?

Courtesy, objectivity and professionalism are the fundamental principles for conducting the interview. It is important that all the parties be put at ease and encouraged to understand both the confidentiality and the seriousness of the investigation. They must know who is involved, how the process works and what the outcomes might be. It may become necessary to use legal terms but remember this is a sensitive organisational investigation, not a TV courtroom drama. Employees should be encouraged to attend accompanied by someone else, as it will help them to relax and give them someone with whom to share reflections later. It is also a statutory right to be accompanied by a colleague or trade union representative when raising a grievance. All of those involved are entitled to have representation, be it a colleague, a harassment officer or a trade union representative.

If any of the parties are disabled reasonable adjustments should be made to enable them to use the procedure, for example:

- having a supporter or carer accompany them, e.g. a signer if the employee is deaf;
- ensuring the room is accessible and there is an accessible toilet available nearby;
- providing any documentation in alternative format, e.g. large print.

The overall purpose of the interviews is to establish what happened, why and how the respective parties view the incident – to gather the facts but not to extend the accusations.

Complainant/victim

- Ask what happened.
- Establish the unwelcome extent of the alleged behaviour.
- Establish the nature/role/status of the harasser.
- Establish the duration of the alleged behaviour.
- Establish the extent of the alleged behaviour. (Does the harasser/respondent treat everyone the same?)
- Establish the context in which the alleged behaviour occurred.
- Get some idea of the emotional/physical state of the complainant.

Harasser/respondent

- Ask what happened.
- Establish his or her perception of his or her own behaviour.
- Establish his or her perception of the complainant's behaviour.
- Get some idea of the emotional/physical state of the respondent.

Witnesses

- Establish their relationship with the complainant.
- Establish their relationship with the respondent.

- Establish any concerns over repercussions and retribution from either party.

- Identify any facts from their evidence.

Coming to a decision

The investigator must be reasonably satisfied that the incident took place. Both parties should be notified in writing when a decision has been reached. If the complaint is upheld, then about any disciplinary action should be taken as soon as possible. It is advisable to inform the person making the complaint whether their complaint has been upheld or not, but not to tell them about any disciplinary sanction applied. This is because this is confidential to the accused person. If the organisation has a major problem with bullying and harassment and is attempting to stamp it out, they can of course publish data on the number of complaints raised, upheld and the outcomes, provided individual confidentiality is maintained.

Remember to allow the complainant the opportunity to appeal if they are unhappy with the way the procedure has been conducted.

Potential outcomes

Some examples of possible outcomes are as follows:

- The allegations are unfounded.

- The case is resolved informally, perhaps involving training and counselling for either or both parties.

- The parties agree to go to mediation.

- The bully or harasser is transferred within the organisation.

- Disciplinary action is taken against the bully or harasser.
- Formal action under a capability procedure is taken against the bully or harasser.
- The complainant is transferred at their instigation
- The bully or harasser is dismissed.

While some policies stipulate that if a complaint is upheld then disciplinary action must follow, this is not always the most effective means of resolving the problem. Each case will depend on its own unique circumstances, including the seriousness of the actions, the accused person's perception of what has happened, whether there is a history of complaints, how long the bullying or harassment has existed and the impact on the complainant. For example, it may be more appropriate to provide the accused with coaching on how to adopt a more varied management style rather than just imposing a disciplinary warning where the manager is struggling to manage. In other situations where there has been a particularly serious case of bullying or harassment, it may be appropriate to dismiss the perpetrator for gross misconduct, provided it has been made clear to all employees that this is a potential penalty.

What happens next?

In many cases a successful resolution can be achieved at the end of informal discussions or a formal investigation. For some organisations facing what may seem to be the impossible or improbable outcome – the two parties working together in harmony again – mediation may be the means to a solution. Some organisations may even consider mediation without moving to any formal investigation as they feel it will save money and time. It may also 'save face' for those involved, most of whom will be glad of a way out that stops the bullying and harassment.

Mediation

Mediation helps the parties to agree a course of action and a solution, but it must be adapted to the organisation. Mediation has been used in the business world for many years, usually to close a deal, be it sales or compensation when the two parties can't agree. Its use in employment issues is relatively new but growing.

How does mediation work?

The mediator is a facilitator and manages the process, not the content. Their purpose is to find a solution acceptable to both parties that is voluntary and allows each to retain dignity. The mediator is not the decision-maker but helps the parties in dispute to reach an understanding and agreement for future working relationships. They do this by helping identify the parties' respective interests (that is their real concerns) and distinguishing these from their positions (what the person is saying), for example:

> *'I don't bother going to lunch in the canteen, that lot are too cliquey'* (position)

could mean:

> *'I feel excluded; I want to feel part of the team'* (interest)

The setting up of the mediation process needs to be undertaken carefully so that the parties understand how it works. There needs to be a voluntary agreement that all parties will abide by the course of action and the solution agreed. The process is without prejudice and all notes must be destroyed when it ends. Confidentiality is paramount in both the agreement and in the independent and joint meetings with the parties involved. The mediator must have immunity, and should not be called as a witness.

Who does it?

It is best to have someone from outside the organisation to gain the most objectivity and trust, for example a professional mediator or an independent consultant. For larger organisations, it is possible to train in-house mediators who are able to work in different areas of the organisation where there can be no compromise of their impartiality.

What happens?

A suggested four-step approach can be found in Appendix 1.

Mediation should take no longer than one day if the parties really want a solution, although in long-standing or complex cases they can take place over several days.

Implementing mediation into your policy

Write the mediation procedure into your policy; it is a good idea to allow the option of mediation to be taken up at the beginning of the process before matters become formalised. It can also be used as an option within the formal process if both parties decide that resolution can be better reached that way.

The procedure should include methods of monitoring and enforcing mediation agreements, and identify the nature of the

Case Study

A senior director in a medium-sized organisation had problems with two employees. Their work was specialised and involved the two employees working closely together with health and safety being a primary consideration. One of the employees was the supervisor of the other. Unfortunately working relationships between the two were rapidly worsening, with neither communicating directly with the other. Matters had come to a head and the two employees had come to blows. This had been dealt with under the disciplinary procedure and would normally lead to dismissal for gross misconduct. However, the director did not want to lose either of the employees as they would be hard to replace, and he was conscious that one of them had previously complained that the other was very difficult to work with and felt he was being bullied.

The director therefore engaged an external mediator to try and resolve the conflict between the two. The mediator ensured that both employees understood what was involved in the process and that they were happy to have her as mediator. She then met with them initially on an individual basis to listen to their respective perspectives on their working relationships before arranging for them to meet face to face. Due to the long-standing feud between the two, it took several meetings over a couple of weeks to get the employees to acknowledge their differences and come up with ways they could work together. The mediator helped them by making suggestions and asking pertinent questions. At the end of the process the two had a much better understanding of each other and a written action plan to implement. Six months later, when the mediator checked on progress, the director was happy to report that the two now worked together effectively and whenever problems arose, they returned to the action plan to remind themselves how best to resolve them.

---

mediator, that is whether they are external to the organisation, and, if internal, say how he or she will be trained. It should say where meetings will take place ensuring that the facilities are top quality and that the administration runs smoothly, and state who will be responsible for managing the times, dates, details of cases, etc. Finally, it is a good idea to elicit union cooperation where necessary.

And afterwards?

Where the resulting action involves separating the parties to the complaint, it is the harasser who should be moved, transferred or suspended, not the complainant. Sometimes the complainant requests a transfer and this should be accommodated.

Even where the complaint is not upheld, there may still be such bad feeling between the parties because of the accusation that some change in their working location or relationship should occur to allow the matter to be forgotten.

In all cases everything possible should be done to avoid further bullying or harassment and the complainant should be given a written undertaking that he or she will not be victimised or suffer further detriment.

Finally, we should remember that there may be instances where it is a third party who has raised the alarm with respect to bullying and sexual harassment. Surveys show that not only do employees find themselves victims, as many, if not more, find themselves witnesses to bullying and harassment. It is vital that any third-party observer alerts others so that the suspected behaviour can be investigated. Where bullying and sexual harassment have been seen to happen but the victim will not make a complaint, it might still be possible to counsel the perpetrators with a view to enabling them to see the impact of their actions on others. If people can harass one individual, then there is a good chance they may harass others. Investigations prompted by a third party might reveal other current or past victims who could be encouraged to come forward.

Monitoring and evaluation

Statistical data

In order to monitor and evaluate progress records should be kept of the:

- number of cases;
- type of cases;
- duration of cases;
- decisions made;
- follow-up mechanisms used.

It is also useful to look at:

- labour turnover in all business units or departments;
- sickness records.

Even the most simple statistics produced from this monitoring will reveal any trend in the number and type of cases and should reassure interested parties that they are being dealt with. This can be further conveyed by looking at similar figures from other organisations in your company's sector or of your organisation's size.

Financial data

Analysis of the figures produced will easily lend itself to expression in terms of manpower utilisation which can then be costed. There may also be costs associated with the solutions – redeployment or relocation at best and, at worst, compensation, an employment tribunal or out-of-court settlement.

This information will be invaluable if you have to justify to the holder of the purse strings the continued use or introduction of policy and procedures.

Surveys and exit interviews

Information showing the presence and extent of bullying and sexual harassment can be gleaned by means other than the analysis of cases. Surveys and exit interviews are also very useful tools in this respect.

Surveys, when carefully designed, can gauge the extent of the problem, the major issues and, if cleverly worded, how strongly employees feel about what should be done. This can be gauged, for example, from the response to the question: 'What did you do about it?' A subsequent question should be asked: 'If you didn't do anything about it, why not?' Such questions can provide valuable qualitative data. People who feel strongly will make a complaint; those who don't will ignore the matter or explain what stopped them, for example 'fear of being ostracised' or 'no one to complain to'.

Exit interviews serve as a major vehicle in providing information about the organisation's culture and management, values and practices. Always conducted in confidence with a person who is not from the work department, these interviews can elicit frank and open comments that an individual may have been too afraid to bring up during his or her employment.

With all of these monitoring techniques it is important to remember that they should be applied regularly and given prominence at organisational level and publicised to employees. This will encourage good behaviour to continue, and bad (unacceptable) behaviour to stop.

In addition to compiling facts and figures, it is also important to evaluate the way in which investigations are carried out and, in particular, the way the panel operates in evaluating information and reaching its decision. It is a good idea to use past cases as tools for training investigators and panel members, highlighting better ways of working and encouraging best practice. The cases can also be used in general management training and development and for the training of counsellors.

Your target should be to have no cases.

There is a constant danger that procedures and incidents will excite the mind and generate activity from which, although one case may be settled, nothing is really learned.

All aspects of bullying and sexual harassment must be reviewed and evaluated to ensure that everything that can be done has been done; the decisions reached are the right ones; the actions taken on the basis of those decisions are appropriate; and that the procedure is picking up and dealing with all cases. This requires quantitative and qualitative evaluation at various stages, and against both internal and external benchmarks.

5

How can I help people enact the policies and procedures?

Awareness-raising

Two main issues arise here:

- Do employees know what bullying and harassment are?
- Does the organisation know the extent of bullying and harassment?

A variety of techniques can be used to raise awareness, including:

- surveys and audits;
- leaflets and pamphlets, posters and signs;
- workshops;
- confidential helpline and equality network;
- confidential, regular open 'surgery' or harassment victim advice network;
- annual summary of cases provided to the board/JCC;
- staff ombudsman;
- employee charter;
- statement in letters of appointment and contracts of employment;
- induction packs and training;

- management debriefing;
- training;
- training!
- training!!

An important aspect of any change in attitude requires everyone in the workforce to understand just what bullying and sexual harassment are. Perceptions vary, but most employers and external bodies would agree that the descriptors in Table 5.1 are acceptable. The table also indicates some of the differences between the two, which can be a reason for treating them as separate issues.

Table 5.1   Descriptors of harassment and bullying

Harassment	Workplace bullying
Harassment has a strong physical component, e.g. contact and touch in all its forms, intrusion into personal space and possessions, damage to possessions such as a person's work.	Bullying is primarily psychological, e.g. criticism, but may become physical at a later stage, especially with male bullies though rarely with female bullies.
Harassment tends to focus on the individual because of what he or she is (e.g. black, disabled, etc.).	Anyone will do, especially if they are competent, popular and vulnerable.
Harassment is usually linked to sex, race, prejudice, discrimination, etc.	Sex, race and gender play little or no part; it's usually discrimination on the basis of competence.
Harassment may consist of a single incident, a few incidents or many incidents.	Bullying is rarely restricted to a single incident and tends to be an accumulation of many small incidents.
The person being harassed knows almost straightaway that he or she is being harassed.	The person being bullied may not realise for weeks or months that he or she is being bullied – until there is a moment of enlightenment.

| Table 5.1 | Descriptors of harassment and bullying (cont'd) |

Harassment	Workplace bullying
There is often an element of possession, e.g. stalking.	Phase one of bullying is control and subjugation; when this fails phase two is an attempt to eliminate the victim.
Often the harassment is for peer approval, bravado, the 'macho' image.	Bullying tends to be secret and behind closed doors with no witnesses.
Harassment takes place both in and out of work.	Bullying takes place mostly at work.

Adapted from Tim Field's *Bully OnLine* website.

Using surveys

Why?

Many of the organisations claiming to have no bullying or sexual harassment do nothing about trying to discover it. A wise move, you might think: one problem fewer to bother about! As one employer put it, 'We have no company policy relating to this, but this does not mean that I am so naive as to think bullying does not occur in some instances.'

The CIPD 2004 *Managing Conflict at Work* survey found that: 'By far the largest single group of employers reporting an increase in bullying in the past two years state that this is due to increasing employee awareness of the issue.' It won't go away, so organisations need to be proactive or when it does emerge it could do as much damage as a tidal wave. If you conduct a survey, you'll be in control and ready to respond.

How?

Questionnaires are the best method. They are short, anonymous and confidential, and you can promise respondents that you will publish a résumé of the findings.

An example of the kind of questions you might ask is given here in Figure 5.1. Under no circumstances should the respondent be encouraged to give actual names at this stage.

Figure 5.1   Sample questionnaire on bullying.

- *Have you experienced bullying or harassment at work?*
- *Have you ever been subject to any of the following behaviours and found them to be offensive and unwanted?*
  - Innuendoes?
  - Staring?
  - Gestures?
  - Display of pornographic materials?
  - Physical abuse or intimidation?
  - Threat to job security?
- *What kind of employee exhibited this behaviour?*
  - A manager?
  - A colleague?
  - Someone who works for you?
- *Has a customer or client ever subjected you to unwanted behaviour?*
- *How often has this happened?*

Figure 5.1 Sample questionnaire on bullying (*cont'd*).

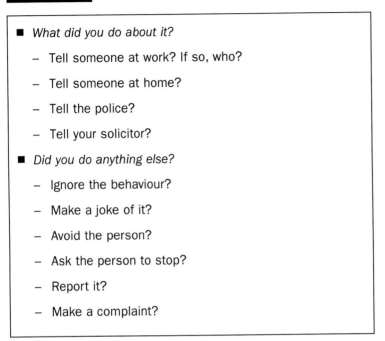

- *What did you do about it?*
  - Tell someone at work? If so, who?
  - Tell someone at home?
  - Tell the police?
  - Tell your solicitor?
- *Did you do anything else?*
  - Ignore the behaviour?
  - Make a joke of it?
  - Avoid the person?
  - Ask the person to stop?
  - Report it?
  - Make a complaint?

What then?

When the completed questionnaires have been returned you should:

- analyse the findings;
- report them to the organisation;
- if instances are reported, be prepared to listen and offer support for individuals to come forward;
- design and implement policy and procedures to deal with the instances if you haven't already done so;
- take it seriously.

Employees should not have to seek information about what constitutes bullying and harassment, or about what can be done about it. Nor should they be unaware of how their behaviour might be unacceptable and where they can seek help.

Counselling

Counselling is recommended at two main stages:

- to enable the victim to establish the extent of his or her case and to stand up to the harasser;
- to support both victim and harasser when they return to a 'normal' working relationship. (This is especially important if the case is not proven.)

Counselling is a positive process that can help to protect the individual within an organisation as well as foster a climate of trust and openness. The counsellor must be:

- respected;
- well regarded;
- trusted;
- credible;
- well trained.

The process must enable:

- the issues to be identified and clarified;
- the reliability and status of reports of the perceived behaviour to be checked out;

- the victim to overcome fear;
- the victim to overcome embarrassment;
- the victim to look for solutions;
- the victim to manage the situation more effectively;
- the victim to regain self-esteem;
- the victim to gain more self-reliance and overcome his or her feeling of helplessness;
- the victim to obtain support in seeing through his or her decisions and enacting the solutions.

This is achieved by:

- establishing whether the victim would confront the harasser in order to:
  - express how that person's behaviour is making him or her feel;
  - give a statement of fact;
  - be explicit (avoid using euphemisms that might be misunderstood);
- role-playing to help the individual rehearse what he or she wants to say;
- encouraging the victim to be objective, because he or she may want to make a formal complaint at a later stage;
- encouraging the victim to imagine how his or her work environment would change if the bullying and sexual harassment ceased:
  - what would be improved;
  - what would be the benefit of taking control and changing the circumstances;

- considering whether the individual would benefit from assertiveness training;

- helping in the evaluation of options;

- helping the victim to evaluate in advance his or her reactions if things do not work out as he or she had hoped.

Introducing a counselling service

Some issues to consider include the following:

- Will employees believe that it is there to help? Will trade unions support it and see it as impartial?

- Will managers believe it will help them to manage rather than 'mollycoddle' 'weak' staff and foster absenteeism?

- How will it be structured? Where will it be located? How much will it cost?

- What type of control should there be? How will confidentiality be assured?

Training

Recognising and dealing with bullying and sexual harassment are not behaviours that come easily to most people. It is essential that knowledge, skills and attitudes are fostered in the organisation to give employees at all levels the confidence and drive to deal with issues, or indeed prevent them from arising. Different individuals have different learning styles which must be taken into consideration, and different aspects of the subject matter may be better dealt with through different training techniques. Some outline suggestions are given here.

The main groups of people to consider are:

- individual employees;
- supervisors, line managers and senior managers;
- professional counsellors and 'buddies';
- panel members hearing the case;
- personnel department staff.

These cover the complete spectrum of sections or departments in the organisation. The things they need to know about will vary, but will include:

- the policy and procedures;
- names, location and function of counsellors and 'buddies';
- recognition of a problem, real or potential, and skills in revealing the problem;
- listening skills;
- counselling skills;
- skills in investigating the problems;
- knowledge of legislation and best practice.

Figure 5.2 indicates what training is needed for key players and shows the depth of knowledge, understanding and skill required.

With this information in mind it will be easy for the organisation to plan and deliver the topic using appropriate methods and working with those who most need the skills and knowledge.

Other sources of training include:

- the TUC, which provides programmes for trade union officials and members;

Figure 5.2 Training needed for key players

	Policy and procedures	Names, location and function of counsellors	Recognition of real or potential problem	Revealing the problem	Listening	Counselling	Investigation skills	Knowledge of legislation and best practice	What happens next?
Personnel staff	✓✓✓	✓✓✓	✓✓✓	✓✓	✓✓✓	✓✓	✓✓✓	✓✓✓	✓✓✓
Individual employees	✓✓✓	✓✓✓	✓✓✓	✓✓✓				✓	✓
Buddy	✓✓✓	✓✓✓	✓	✓	✓			✓	
Supervisor/line managers	✓✓✓	✓✓✓	✓✓✓	✓✓✓	✓✓✓	✓	✓✓	✓✓	✓✓✓
Senior managers	✓✓✓	✓	✓	✓✓	✓✓✓	✓	✓✓	✓✓	✓
Counsellors	✓✓✓	✓✓✓	✓✓✓	✓✓	✓✓✓	✓✓✓		✓	✓
Panel members	✓✓✓	✓	✓✓✓	✓	✓✓✓	✓	✓✓	✓✓✓	✓✓

- the Work Foundation (see Appendix 4 for details), which publishes a pack that includes a book, video and advice on how to develop a training session.

About the techniques

Written

Information posters and handbooks need to be graphic, to the point, and emphasise what constitutes bullying and sexual harassment.

Seminars and group discussions

These need to be in small groups, discrete and not too lengthy. They should serve to further explore the application of policy and procedures, including how to recognise and reveal instances of harassment and bullying. They may be led by someone with confidence and full knowledge of *all* the range of topics – perhaps a line manager, counsellor or member of the personnel staff.

Case studies

These need to be short and to the point and usable within the seminar/group discussion session. If they reflect real events and participants get to know 'what really happened in the end' after they have passed judgement, they will improve people's motivation to listen. If they are too remote from your own business context, you will hear cries of 'that would never happen here'. Again, a well-informed trainer/facilitator is needed to guide participants through the case and summarise conclusions.

Role-play

This is something with which most people feel uncomfortable. Case studies are much 'safer': you only have to give your opinion – you do not have to 'do it'. Nevertheless, we want to encourage certain types of behaviour here and we want participants to know what it feels like to be bullied, to be wrongly accused of sexual harassment, to sit on a panel, or to try to broach the subject with someone whom you feel may be involved.

Participants will feel uneasy and self-conscious, so confidentiality and a very professional trainer/facilitator is required. Twenty-five years of teaching interview skills through role-play has led me to believe that it is the best way to achieve results, but participants take some persuading. It is better to get it wrong in front of colleagues in a safe situation than to 'blow' a potentially dangerous situation!

This role-play should really grow from the comfort and detachment of the case study.

Debriefing

Whenever an instance of harassment or bullying occurs, it should be used as a vehicle for learning. Once the case has been dealt with, and subject to any confidentiality felt necessary, the sharing of the experience will be an invaluable lesson for the future and will give confidence to all involved that they can deal with it. Again, the session should be led by a skilled trainer/facilitator and the manager of the department concerned (provided of course the manager was neither victim nor aggressor). If you can get the victim to contribute, it will help people's understanding. If an individual is found to have been wrongly accused of harassment, it would also be extremely helpful to hear about his or her experience. The more knowledge we have about situations, the better we are able to learn about and deal with them. Training staff to recognise and deal with bullying and harassment should be ongoing and should be part of the induction and basic training of all staff. Changes in policy or procedures need to be dealt with as they happen.

In the event that you are fortunate enough to have no 'real' cases, managers should have their knowledge refreshed and their skills polished every 12–18 months. Posters and other publications will keep the information alive for most other employees. Figure 5.3 shows some of the different techniques that might be used.

People need to have the right knowledge, skills and behaviours to be able to prevent bullying and harassment in the workplace. They cannot be expected to develop any of these if the organisation is not willing to provide the opportunities for training.

Figure 5.3 Training techniques involved in dealing with bullying and harassment

	Written publications, e.g. posters, handbooks	Seminars and discussion groups	Case files, real or fictitious	Role-play	Debriefing
Policy and procedures	✓	✓	✓		
Names, location and function of counsellors	✓				
Problem recognition	✓	✓	✓	✓	✓
Problem revelation	✓	✓	✓	✓	✓
Listening	✓	✓	✓	✓	✓
Counselling	✓	✓	✓	✓	✓
Investigating	✓	✓	✓	✓	✓
Legislation and best practice	✓	✓			✓
What happens next			✓	✓	✓

6

Where does it all end?

As a personnel professional or line manager you have several important responsibilities, including contributing to the success of your organisation in achieving its business objectives and maintaining the dignity and quality of working life for the people it employs. This is a constantly challenging if unenviable task. How do you know what is acceptable and what is changeable?

The manager has a right to manage

The role of the manager is one of type, trait, contingency or even a mixture of all three. The manager's job is often fragmented and ill defined: in many organisations a manager's job description is like a piece of string – as long as it needs to be! Certain generic qualities persist, however, and today's organisation needs managers who are:

- flexible – coping with an ever-changing environment and a broad and sometimes contradictory set of demands;

- supportive – acting as coaches and mentors rather than as directors or conductors;

- responsive – to customers, other sections of the organisation, peers, colleagues and subordinates;

- resilient – constantly regrouping, communicating and persuading others;

- visionary – providing leadership, leadership, leadership.

Managers in all organisations must be seen to be performing in certain core activities:

- achieving results;

- working through people;

- planning and organising;

- communicating;

- evaluating and monitoring;

- getting home occasionally.

The manager has to exercise power to carry out his or her job. Even in organisations that have 'flattened' themselves with the restructuring roller there will still be some people who wield power and authority. According to Hofstede (1994) a small power distance, typified by flatter structures, less hierarchy and more matrix management, will reduce the likelihood of harassment. However, in any business the manager's role is to manage and organisations must clarify the limits of power and authority for both the manager and the managed.

The organisation has a right to control people's behaviour

Organisations too are in a privileged position when it comes to exercising power and authority over employees, and they should share the understanding of that position. Organisational culture shapes the behaviour of employees and they, in turn, shape the way the organisation performs. Culture is a soft, holistic concept, also described as the psychological assets of an organisation, which can be used to predict what will happen to its financial assets in five years' time.

Culture includes deep-set beliefs about work organisation, authority, reward and control, and it seems that some organisations are just asking for trouble. *Should the existing culture be allowed to persist if it breaks the law or treats groups or individuals without respect or dignity or, worse still, with degradation and humiliation?*

The armed services, police and fire services are good examples of culture and climate that present major difficulties. These are made worse by the fact that women in non-traditional environments are subject to a higher rate of harassment than women in other areas. Unused to employing women, such organisations do little to prepare for their arrival. Women moving into a previously all-male domain feel isolated and uneasy. Organisations do not change their culture suddenly, and firm and positive steps 'from the top' are now having to be taken. What has taken decades to evolve, and has lasted for further decades, may take decades to change – if it ever does.

The armed forces have a culture where conformity is the norm and accepting different ways of 'doing things around here' does not go comfortably hand in hand with history. The prejudice that has to be overcome by women in these male-dominated cultures is illustrated by the following remarks:

The Wrens probably suffer sexual harassment. It is what you would expect in a working place with a lot of virile men. (Royal Navy admiral)

The politically correct creeps behind this ludicrous action are stupid. (Royal Navy admiral)

> The sub-officer referred to her as a 'cow' and told her to get a job in the kitchen. (Evidence from an industrial tribunal case brought by a female firefighter)

The City, it is said, is an example of an organisation with a very high level of bullying. Intense pressure coupled with high numbers of young recruits who lack interpersonal skills and experience of the work environment easily leads to bullying by older staff with more work experience. It is suggested that an individual's behaviour is perpetuated in a kind of reiterative loop as each group moves up the organisation.

Tim Field describes phenomena that he calls 'corporate bullying' or 'organisational bullying'. These are characteristic of types of employers who abuse employees with impunity, knowing that the law is weak and jobs are scarce. Actions typical of such organisations include:

- coercing employees to work 60–80 hours a week on a regular basis, then making life hell for (or dismissing) anyone who objects;

- dismissing anyone who looks like having a breakdown through stress because it is cheaper to pay unfair dismissal costs than personal injury breakdown claims;

- deeming any employee suffering from stress to be weak and inadequate;

- 'encouraging' employees (with promises of promotion and/or threats of disciplinary action) to fabricate complaints about their colleagues.

Employees should look out for themselves

If people in organisations shape the culture, and if a manager's behaviour is strongly influenced by the expectations of peers and subordinates, then 'people power' might be thought sufficient to override possible bullying and sexual harassment. Evidence shows that this is not the case, for several reasons:

- job security may be at risk;
- individuals are isolated, believing it is happening only to them;
- no one likes confrontation;
- victims do not believe they have the right to complain;
- they hope it will stop;
- they do not know how to complain;
- they believe that even if they do complain, nothing will be done.

In environments where bullying is the norm, most people will eventually become either bullies or victims. There may be some bystanders, but most will be sucked in. For the individual it is all about survival; you can either adopt bullying tactics yourself and thus survive by not becoming a victim, or you stand up against bullying and refuse to join in. This latter approach frequently leads to individuals being bullied, harassed, victimised and scapegoated until they fall ill or leave.

Individuals can cope only if the organisation supports them.

And if the business is thriving?

The order books may be full at the moment, the service demand may be stretching the workforce to capacity, but how long is it going to last? Business today in the public or private sector is a rollercoaster ride. Employees are your most flexible and enduring resource.

If you want to get value for money, value them as human beings and they'll be with you through the downs as well as the ups. If you don't value them, then it won't be long before someone blows the whistle and your business just might not survive.

Finally ...

This book asks many questions and suggests some of the answers. The questions are a prompt for you, and your answers will be defined by circumstances as they exist for you. Use the questions to get the answers that are best for you and always keep this thought in mind:

If any behaviour in your organisation results in treating individuals or groups without respect or dignity or, worse still, with degradation *and* humiliation, then whether it breaks the law or not, it must stop.

Appendix 1
Procedures

Complaints checklist

Does your bullying and harassment complaints procedure comply with the new standard statutory grievance procedure (below), as a minimum?

Step 1: Statement of grievance

- The employee must set out the grievance in writing and send the statement or copy of it to the employer.

Step 2: Meeting

- The employer must invite the employee to attend a meeting to discuss the grievance.
- The meeting must not take place unless –
  - the employee has informed the employer what the basis for the grievance was when he or she made the statement under Step 1 above; and
  - the employer has had a reasonable opportunity to consider his response to that information.

- The employee must take all reasonable steps to attend the meeting.

- After the meeting the employer must inform the employee of his decision as to his response to the grievance and notify the employee of the right to appeal against the decision if the employee is not satisfied with it.

Step 3: Appeal

- If the employee does wish to appeal, he or she must inform the employer.

- If the employee informs the employer of his or her wish to appeal, the employer must invite the employee to attend a further meeting.

- After the appeal meeting the employer must inform the employee of his final decision.

Bullying and harassment procedure checklist

You must make your staff aware of your procedure, either by giving them individual copies or by posting a summary in a public place. It should always state the following:

- an initial informal option, followed by a formal process if necessary;

- how to make the complaint;

- options of who to make the complaint to;

- how the matter will be investigated;

- who will conduct the investigation;

- the timetable for investigation;
- employees' rights to representation;
- details of the appeals procedure;
- the requirement for confidentiality;
- whether, and in what circumstances, mediation is available;
- the remedial sanctions which may be invoked against the bully or harasser.

Informal procedure

- Are there trained volunteers or counsellors?
- Do employees know where to locate them?
- Do employees know what the volunteer/counsellor will and can do?
- Do employees know that they can bring a complaint about something that they have witnessed or even suspect?
- Do line managers understand their responsibility to 'nip problems in the bud'?

Formal procedure

- There is a formal, written complaint identifying harasser and incident(s).
- The complaint is acknowledged in writing on receipt (for example, within two working days).
- The alleged harasser is notified in writing, with full details of the allegations (for example, within two working days).
- All parties are told of their rights of representation.

- A full investigation is made by a panel or independent person (for example, within ten working days).

- The results of the investigation are notified to both parties in writing (for example, within three working days of the findings being agreed).

- Any further action is taken as soon as possible.

- If the complaint is upheld, the complainant is given a written undertaking that no further victimisation will take place.

- There is a right to appeal if the complainant is unhappy with the outcome or the way the case has been dealt with.

- Comprehensive records are kept of the investigation, its findings and subsequent actions.

- A nominated person reviews the situation at a later date (for example, six months later).

Conducting an investigation checklist

Preliminary points

- Decide who will be responsible for booking rooms and administrative arrangements.

- Check that the investigator is neutral and free from any potential claims of bias.

- Check on likely timescale and availability of parties, investigator and witnesses.

The investigation

The investigator should:

- explain the purpose and procedure of the investigation to each party;
- check that the parties are represented if they wish;
- listen to the complainant;
- ask relevant questions to identify the facts;
- put evidence of the complaint to the alleged bully/harasser;
- listen to their explanation;
- ask questions to establish facts;
- collect written statements from all parties and witnesses;
- give the statements to the parties and witnesses to sign as a true and accurate copy;
- note any amendments or disagreements;
- make a decision;
- notify the parties in writing;
- make recommendations for the next step(s).

Mediation checklist

A suggested approach to mediation is outlined below.

Step 1

- *Explain the purpose and process* of mediation to both parties: that it is intended to achieve a win/win outcome and future focus, that it is voluntary and any party can opt out at any time and that the process is confidential.

- *Emphasise that the process is about moving on*, not looking back, although it needs to be acknowledged that what has happened in the past has led to the present conflict.

- *Meet with each party individually* in order to hear what their perception of the 'problem' is and identify whether there are acknowledged 'facts'. Some discussion on effective listening skills may be needed.

- *Ensure the parties are happy to go ahead.*

Step 2

- *Arrange to meet the parties in a neutral venue.* Choice of venue is important; it should be private, confidential, without interruptions and away from the normal working area. It is a good idea to meet outside of the workplace if possible in mutually agreed territory. A break-out room should be available if anyone needs to adjourn and wants a side meeting with the mediator.

- *Explain the ground rules.* Parties should: listen when someone is talking, not interrupt as each person will have an opportunity to ask questions and put their views, avoid making personal comments and avoid aggressive behaviour, etc. Remind the parties of confidentiality.

- *Explain the role of the mediator.* The mediator is non-judgemental and impartial, and is there to help the parties to gain a future focus.

- *Ask* which party would like to start. If there is disagreement the mediator should make a suggestion.

- *Ask each party in turn to put forward their views and feelings* regarding the problem. The other party (or parties) listen. They may ask questions when the other person has finished. Each person is asked to focus on how they feel by using 'I' rather than 'you'. For example, 'I feel *x* when you ....' rather than 'you' make me feel *x* when you ....'

- *Ask probing questions* in order to identify issues and distinguish them from each party's position.
- *Acknowledge* expressed feelings.
- *Be sensitive* to non-verbal communication.
- *Adjourn* if any party becomes upset, angry, etc.
- *Ask* each party what they want as an outcome.
- *Summarise* each party's interests.

Step 3

- *Ask* each party to offer suggestions to resolve the conflict.
- *Suggest* solutions, usually through questioning.
- *Each party agrees solutions.*
- *If there are disagreements* explore why and try to move towards mutually acceptable solutions.
- *Get agreement* on action plan.

Step 4

- *Follow up meeting(s)* by confirming outcome and action plan in writing to each party and anyone else it was agreed would have access to the outcome.
- *Monitor* progress at an agreed later date.

Appendix 2
Self-assessment

You might find it interesting to glance at these questionnaires, just to get a feel of how you and/or your organisation might rate. The questions are generalised and would not be suitable for a thorough organisational survey. These questionnaires are included here just for browsing.

Are you at risk of becoming (or are you already) a bully?

This self-assessment test is designed to get you to look at your behaviour in an honest and analytical way. If you are prone to behaving in a certain way, your behaviour could be construed by others as intimidating or aggressive.

Please tick the box that best describes your response. Total your scores and see if you are in danger of being a bully!

A = Usually   **B** = Sometimes   **C** = Rarely

1. I like to work in the 'here and now', I prefer not to think ahead.

   A ❑   B ❑   C ❑

2. I find it hard to deal with failure, especially in a personal sense.

   A ❑   B ❑   C ❑

---

3. I do not have a good memory and tend to forget things easily.

A ❏   B ❏   C ❏

4. I can be very selective in what I remember, and tend to filter out things which I find unpleasant or difficult to deal with.

A ❏   B ❏   C ❏

5. I can be economical with the truth at times.

A ❏   B ❏   C ❏

6. I believe that you have to look after number one in this life.

A ❏   B ❏   C ❏

7. When I make a decision I stick with it. I do not reverse or overturn my decisions.

A ❏   B ❏   C ❏

8. I am not a good listener.

A ❏   B ❏   C ❏

9. I feel that people should be able to take a joke. There are too many people who are oversensitive.

A ❏   B ❏   C ❏

10. I demand high standards from others. I don't believe that people work hard enough.

A ❏   B ❏   C ❏

11. I try and praise people, but end up pulling them up for their shortcomings.

A ❏   B ❏   C ❏

12. I believe that others have more strengths and talents than myself.

A ❑   B ❑   C ❑

13. I do not believe that I can fulfil my dreams and become as successful as others.

A ❑   B ❑   C ❑

14. I think that my job is much harder than other people's. They have an easier time of it than me.

A ❑   B ❑   C ❑

15. There is no need to thank people for the work they do.

A ❑   B ❑   C ❑

16. I would not dream of taking someone else's work and passing it off as my own.

A ❑   B ❑   C ❑

17. It is acceptable to shift the goal posts without consulting staff.

A ❑   B ❑   C ❑

18. I use sarcasm and/or criticism to get people to do what I want.

A ❑   B ❑   C ❑

19. My relationship with work colleagues tends to be rather superficial.

A ❑   B ❑   C ❑

20. It is important that I behave in different ways towards my boss, my peers and my juniors.

A ❑   B ❑   C ❑

21. I suffer from mood swings, usually on a daily basis.

A ❑   B ❑   C ❑

22. I do not delegate well to my junior staff. I am not happy to give the responsibility.

A ❑   B ❑   C ❑

23. I like to keep an eye on people to make sure that they are doing things to my satisfaction.

A ❑   B ❑   C ❑

24. I believe that the way I do things is the right way.

A ❑   B ❑   C ❑

25. I believe that if you apologise to someone it can be seen as a sign of weakness.

A ❑   B ❑   C ❑

26. I don't feel the need to use positive language and statements when talking over work issues with colleagues.

A ❑   B ❑   C ❑

27. While I try to treat all my staff fairly, it is inevitable that I will have favourites.

A ❑   B ❑   C ❑

28. I suffer from indecisiveness.

A ❑   B ❑   C ❑

29. I am not always happy to take on extra responsibility. I see it as an imposition.

A ❑   B ❑   C ❑

Scoring:

For each	A ☑	Score 2	Total	☐
For each	B ☑	Score 1	Total	☐
For each	C ☑	Score 0	Total	☐
Grand total				☐

Do you work for a bullying organisation?

This questionnaire looks at some of the factors which have been identified through research as being indicators of a bullying organisation. A culture which promotes or condones aggressive behaviour from its employees will not lead to an effective and efficient organisation. Look at the following statements and judge which apply to yours. Be careful to look at the 'big picture', not just your department. If the statements do apply just to your department, there could potentially be a bullying sub-culture within your company, which may be a result of a particular individual or group of individuals

Please tick the box that best describes your response. Total your scores and see if you work in a bullying organisation.

A = Usually   **B** = Sometimes   **C** = Rarely

30. There is an obvious 'them and us' culture – evidenced by perks such as pay rises and corporate hospitality events.

    A ☐   B ☐   C ☐

31. People skills are not valued as highly as budgetary and accounting skills.

    A ❑   B ❑   C ❑

32. Lip service is paid to the corporate statement that 'people are our greatest asset'.

    A ❑   B ❑   C ❑

33. People who are recruited and promoted tend to be clones of senior management.

    A ❑   B ❑   C ❑

34. Initiative, creativity and diversity are not rewarded. These qualities are perceived as threatening to senior staff.

    A ❑   B ❑   C ❑

35. People will not take risks for the benefit of the company.

    A ❑   B ❑   C ❑

36. Managers do not adopt a consultative approach

    A ❑   B ❑   C ❑

37. Managers are not in touch with the reality of what goes on in the organisation. They stick to plans and objectives when it is obvious to everyone else that they are inappropriate.

    A ❑   B ❑   C ❑

38. People here do not trust each other or work together cooperatively.

    A ❑   B ❑   C ❑

39. When our organisation needs to make staff cutbacks it saves money by manoeuvring people into leaving rather than having to make redundancy payments.

A ☐   B ☐   C ☐

40. People these days are doing the same amount of work (or more) in fewer hours and for less money.

A ☐   B ☐   C ☐

41. People are coerced into not taking holidays or coming back to work when they should still be off sick.

A ☐   B ☐   C ☐

42. Job security is threatened by managers insisting that we work compulsory overtime or unsociable hours. Refusal labels us as troublemakers.

A ☐   B ☐   C ☐

43. There are limited opportunities for career enhancement and development within the organisation.

A ☐   B ☐   C ☐

44. Money is spent on building up the company image but it is difficult to get monies or resources for important situations.

A ☐   B ☐   C ☐

45. This is a stable workforce. There is very little turnover of staff.

A ☐   B ☐   C ☐

46. The number of people taking sick leave has increased recently. A number seem to be off with stress-related problems.

A ☐   B ☐   C ☐

47. There is a pervasive atmosphere of negativity. Suspicion, hypersensitivity and hyper-vigilance are the norm.

A ☐   B ☐   C ☐

48. There is a strong tendency to work in the 'here and now'. Short-term thinking is evident.

A ☐   B ☐   C ☐

49. Morale is low. People do not look forward to coming to work.

A ☐   B ☐   C ☐

50. There is a current trend to move people to short-term contracts from full-time ones.

A ☐   B ☐   C ☐

51. If there is a problem at work it's hard to find someone who is willing to listen and help.

A ☐   B ☐   C ☐

52. Junior staff find it hard to access those higher up the ladder in a rigid hierarchy.

A ☐   B ☐   C ☐

53. There is an unwillingness to accept that bullying and harassment occur. You do not make waves.

A ☐   B ☐   C ☐

Scoring:

For each   A ☑   Score 2   **Total**   ☐

For each   B ☑   Score 1   **Total**   ☐

For each   C ☑   Score 0   **Total**   ☐

Grand total   ☐

Are you at risk of becoming (or are you already) a bully?

Interpreting the scores

- If your score was within the **0–20 points zone**, it is unlikely that your behaviour is bullying. There may be some instances when you are under pressure when you may not behave as well as you would like but it won't be a regular occurrence.

- If your score was within the **21–40 points zone,** you need to be much more aware of your behaviour. This is a warning which suggests you tend to use bullying tactics to get others to do what you want or to ensure that things go your way. Perhaps you are not aware of how you behave impacts on others. If so, you need to look at your behaviour more closely and start taking responsibility for your actions.

- If you scored more than **41 points** you could be in real trouble. High scores within the 41 points zone suggest that you may be insensitive to the needs of others and intolerant of their views. You really need to think hard about changing your behaviour. You may disagree with these statements and believe that what you practise is 'strong management' or that the confrontations with others can be put down to personality clashes. This is unlikely to be so but admitting that you are a bully is not easy. You are the only one who can change your behaviour but you must first recognise it for what it is and accept that it needs to change.

Do you work for a bullying organisation?

Interpreting the scores

- If your score was within the **0–15 points zone**, it is probably the case that your organisation does not have a bullying culture. However, there may be some practices or attitudes which could be improved upon. It is better not to rest on your laurels thinking that all is fine – there is always room for improvement.

- If your score was within the **16–35 points zone**, alarm bells should be ringing. Although these scores are in the medium range, there should be certain behaviours and approaches which give cause for concern. If you responded 'Sometimes' to most of the statements, it could mean that your organisation is heading for trouble. If the relevant issues are not addressed, it could mean that, within a short period of time, you could move into the 35+ points zone.

- If your score totals **35+ points** there is definitely a problem. There is strong evidence that a bullying culture pervades the organisation. It is likely that productivity and efficiency are compromised and that the workforce is demoralised and demotivated. Maybe people will stay because they do not have other alternatives, but many will be actively looking to leave or may already have done so. It is imperative that changes are made, and swiftly. The situation can be turned around, but only with the commitment and dedication of the decision-makers.

Appendix 3
Types of bully and bullying behaviour

From the Bully OnLine website: *www.bullyonline.org*.

There are many manifestations of bullying. Listed below are some of the most common classifications:

Client bullying – where employees are bullied by those whom they serve, e.g. teachers by pupils, nurses by patients or patients' relatives, shop workers by customers, benefits staff by claimants.

Corporate bullying – where the organisation abuses the employee (see Chapter 5): coercing employees to work long hours, spying on employees, deeming any employee suffering from stress as weak and inadequate.

Cyber bullying – misuse of e-mails, 'flame mails', misuse of the Internet or intranet to bully someone at work.

Gang bullying – where there is a serial bully with colleagues, half the people in the gang are happy to behave badly, others are coerced into joining in usually through fear of being the target if they don't.

Hierarchical bullying, peer bullying and upward bullying – 75 per cent of complaints cite being bullied by the line manager, 25 per cent involve bullying by peers and a very small number of cases involve a manager being bullied by a subordinate. Managers today seem especially susceptible to pressure bullying.

Institutional bullying – similar to corporate bullying when behaviour becomes entrenched in the culture and is seen as the norm hence it is not challenged.

Legal bullying – where vexatious legal action is brought against an individual to punish them.

Organisational bullying – a combination of pressure bullying and corporate bullying, this occurs when organisations are struggling to adapt to changing circumstances.

Pressure bullying – where the stress of the moment causes behaviour to deteriorate and when the pressure is removed normal behaviour is resumed. The danger here is that the pressure (especially at work) is constant so the normal behaviour never resumes.

Regulation bullying – where individuals are forced to comply with rules, regulations and procedures even when they are inappropriate, unnecessary or inapplicable.

Residual bullying – the kind of bullying that continues after the serial bully has left: like recruits like and promotes like. This can last for years.

Secondary bullying – this may occur as unwitting bullying that starts when there is a serial bully in the department. The pressure of dealing with the serial bully causes everyone's behaviour to decline.

Serial bullying – here the source of all dysfunction can be traced to one individual. When they leave the department or organisation the bullying stops only to appear in their new place of work. They are likely to be bullies in all aspects of their life, not just at work.

Vicarious bullying – where one party becomes the bully's instrument of harassment and is deceived or manipulated into bullying the other party when the real bully is getting away without blame.

Appendix 4
Useful contacts and sources of further information

Organisations

ACAS
180 Borough High Street
LONDON
SE1 1LW
Tel: 08457 474747 (helpline)
     0207 210 3613 (or local office)

The Andrea Adams Trust
1 Hove Villas
HOVE
East Sussex
BN3 3DH
Tel: 01273 704900

CIPD (Chartered Institute of Personnel and
Development)
151 The Broadway
LONDON
SW19 1JQ
Tel: 020 8971 9000

Citizens' Advice Bureau
Myddleton House
115–123 Pentonville Road
LONDON
N1 9LZ
Tel: 020 7833 2181 (or local office)

Equal Opportunities Commission
Overseas House
Quay Street
MANCHESTER
M3 3HN
Tel: 0161 833 9244

HSE Information Centre
Broad Lane
SHEFFIELD
S3 7HQ
Tel: 0114 289 2345

Industrial Relations Services
18–20 Highbury Place
LONDON
N5 1QP
Tel: 020 7354 5858

The Suzy Lamplugh Trust
PO Box 17818
LONDON
SW14 8WW
Tel: 0208 876 0305

SME Equality Project
Welsh Development Agency
Plas Glyndwr
Kingsway
CARDIFF
CF10 3AH
Tel: 02920 368286
(For free advice for qualifying small businesses in Wales.)

TUC
Congress House
Great Russell Street
LONDON
WC1 3LS
Tel: 020 7636 4030

The Wainwright Trust
Town Farm House
Mill End
Standon
WARE
Herts
SG11 1LP
Tel: 01920 821698

Terri Wiltshire Associates
67 Caereau Road
NEWPORT
South Wales
NP20 4HJ
Tel: 01633 259798

Work Foundation
Robert Hyde House
48 Bryanston Square
London
W1H 7LN
Tel: 020 7479 2000

Websites

An extensive and comprehensive website can be found at:

http://www.bullyonline.org

Other useful websites:

http://www.acas.org.uk
http://www.eoc.org.uk
http://www.equalitydirect.org.uk
http://www.equalta.co.uk

Publications

While the number of publications about bullying and harassment is growing, the range is not huge. The titles below are an indicative list of what is available. Business and HR journals and publications such as *People Management, Personnel Today, Human Resources, Director, Management Today, Professional Manager* and *Edge* often carry articles on the topic.

Books

Adams, A. (1992) *Bullying at Work: How to Overcome It.* London: Virago.

Einarsen, S., Hoel, H., Zapf, D. and Cooper, G. (2003) *Bullying and Emotional Abuse in the Workplace*. London: Taylor & Francis.

Field, T. (1996) *Bully in Sight*. Wantage: Success Unlimited.

Health and Safety Executive (2003) *Real Solutions, Real People*. Sudbury: HSE.

Ishmael, A. (1999) *Harassment, Bullying and Violence at Work*. London: Industrial Society.

Stephens, T. (1999) *Bullying and Sexual Harassment*. London: CIPD.

Research reports and guides

CIPD (2005) *Bullying at Work: Beyond Policies to a Culture of Respect*. London: CIPD.

CIPD (2004) *Managing Conflict at Work: A Survey of the UK and Northern Ireland*. London: CIPD.

Wainright Trust (2004) *Picking Up the Pieces*. Ware, Herts: Wainwright Trust.

References

CIPD (2004) *Managing Conflict at Work: A Survey of the UK and Ireland*. London: CIPD.

Field, Tim (1996) *Bully in Sight*. Wantage: Success Unlimited.

Field, Tim (n.d.) *Bully OnLine*. Available at: *http://www.bullyonline.org*.

Handy, Charles (1985) *Understanding Organisations*. London: Penguin.

Hofstede, G. (1994) *Cultures and Organisations*. London: HarperCollins.

Jay, A. (1967) *Management and Machiavelli*. London: Hodder & Stoughton.

McClelland, D. and Burnham, D. (1976) 'Power: the great motivator', *Harvard Business Review*, March–April.

Index